TALES

YORKSHIRE
COAST

Dalesman

Dalesman Publishing Company Ltd
Stable Courtyard, Broughton Hall,
Skipton, North Yorkshire BD23 3AZ
www.dalesman.co.uk

First published 2001

Text © Arthur Godfrey

Illustrations by Christine Isherwood

A British Library Cataloguing in Publication record
is available for this book

ISBN 1 85568 189 7

Printed by Amadeus Press, Cleckheaton

Contents

A NOTE FROM THE AUTHOR

All of the tales in this little book are factual; the dates, names and places are all real — except, possibly, for one, which I have been unable to verify. Mad Isaac did exist, and he is still remembered by some Scarborough people. But over the harbour wall? I doubt it! Read the story and see what you think.

King's Cruisers versus the Smugglers

In the early 1700s smuggling became a major industry – mainly
because of increased customs duties on imports such as wines, spirits,
tea, lace and tobacco. All of these were high in value, but small in vol-
ume, making them irresistible. On top of this, ships had improved enor-
mously: instead of the cumbersome and slow square-riggers of earlier
times, smugglers could make use of fore-and-aft rigged cutters which
were fast, handy and sea-kindly. The revenue men also used the same
sort of vessel, but theirs were often no match for their quarry. In 1729
there was one such revenue cruiser on duty between Flamborough

Head and Newcastle, an area she could not hope to cover adequately.

Smugglers treated the revenue men and their ships with disdain. For instance, on April 24th, 1777, Captain Mitchell was cruising off Robin Hood's Bay in the revenue cutter *Swallow*, when he fell in with a well-known smuggler called David Browning who "waved him off". Four days later, off Spurn Point, the *Swallow* came across the *Kent,* another well-known smuggler, and again Mitchell deemed it wiser to veer off. Further meetings of this kind took place on the 2nd and 13th of May and in each case the revenue men backed off. They were simply out-gunned and out-manned on each occasion.

During the last week of September that same year, the *Swallow* hailed a smuggling cutter after dark, but did not press the point, and went inshore to anchor off Saltburn. The next morning, to add insult to injury, the smuggling cutter bore down on the revenue cruiser and rammed her, telling the lawmen to clear off or be sunk! The *Swallow* tripped her anchor and beat a hasty retreat!

The story does, however, have a happy ending: both Browning and George Fagg (master of the *Kent)* were finally apprehended by the revenue men. The *Kent* was off Filey when two revenue cutters, *Prince of Wales* and *Royal George,* took her on and a ferocious gun-battle ensued. It seemed at one stage that the smuggler was gaining the upper hand and would escape justice when *HMS Pelican* joined the fray. The battle continued through the night and into the next day when another naval vessel, *HMS Arethusa,* hove into view and the *Kent* finally struck her colours: i.e. surrendered. The prize was taken to Hull where it was found that she was armed with 16 four-pounders, 20 swivel guns, and large quantities of shot. She carried 39 crew (as against the *Swallow*'s 14) and was valued at over £1,400 – a great sum in those days.

Browning, the other thorn in Captain Mitchell's side, was not taken until 1788, after a long chase off the Dorset coast.

The Joy of Steamboats

Steamboat rides from Yorkshire coast ports during the nineteenth century may have seemed a dubious pleasure which holidaymakers were not slow in pointing out. A letter to the *Scarborough Gazette* in September 1858 described steamboats leaving the pier as

" … disgracefully dirty … with grimy sailors spitting about the deck, seasick ladies in need of a female attendant … unprotected ladies falling under the care of the musicians on board, their musical efforts being disregarded, as a better harvest could be reaped by playing stewardess! The method of landing is dangerous and disgusting – and improper for ladies … "

Captain Jeremiah Hudson, owner of the *Fame,* the steamer concerned, wrote a reply which did nothing to advance his cause. He pointed out that

" … many visitors come aboard *Fame* for the express purpose of being well-cleansed with sea-sickness; three sailors are employed for supplying the sick with water, and mopping the decks … one sick lady had been liberally supplied with brandy beforehand, hence her difficulty in disembarking. The spitting sailors are grimy through stoking furnaces, and are washing their mouths out with water … and furthermore, the writer of the complaining letter is henceforth excluded from Captain Hudson's steamboats!"

Jeremiah Hudson appeared in the news again in July 1865, at which time he was captain of the Hull steamer *Sir Colin Campbell.* Southbound from Whitby, he took the vessel too close inshore and struck rocks some five miles south of Robin Hood's Bay, damaging the bottom of the ship. Contemporary reports state that

> " … the passengers were very judiciously kept in ignorance of the accident whilst efforts were being made to stop the rapid influx of water which was flowing through a hole made in her bottom … "

Two ship's carpenters, who were aboard as passengers, were pressed into service and the ship was able to reach Scarborough where she was beached for proper repairs.

Another pleasure steamer found herself in trouble at Whitby within the month. The *Superb*, with Captain John Ford, was approaching the piers when a sailing coble crossed her bows, forcing Ford to take rapid evasive action and resulting in the steamer crashing into the pier. As a result of the damage she sustained, the passengers were obliged to abandon their return trip. The owners of the vessel were displeased and Ford was sacked. This so inflamed him that he wrote to the local newspaper claiming that he had been master of the vessel for eighteen months and this was his first accident! Furthermore, it was clear from his dismissal that the owners believed he ought to have, instead, run down the coble and drowned its occupants! The owners retaliated by writing that Ford's sacking was not connected with the incident but was because he was dirty in appearance and a generally all-round disagreeable person!

John Donkin and Mad Isaac

Scarborough's fishing community was not short of unusual characters, John Donkin being one such. Fishermen could often earn an extra pound or two by offering to guide large vessels into the harbour when bad weather made local knowledge vitally important. However, this meant that the would-be pilot had to be out at sea in the worst of weather. John Donkin would fight his way out of the harbour in terrible weather and would lie in a bight, between the outer pier and the castle foot, awaiting likely customers. The place where he waited is still known today as John Donkin's Bight. For all the risks he took he was certainly a survivor: when the large steamship *SS Amity* ran down a coble in which he was fishing off Robin Hood's Bay in January of 1862 John lived to tell the tale, while his two companions were both drowned.

When stormy weather made it impossible for a sailing vessel to enter the harbour at Scarborough, a huge fire was lit in a brazier at the seaward end of the pier; fishermen were obliged to stay at sea, sometimes for many hours, simply stemming the seas and trying to stay afloat. This warning was known as "burning off" and was naturally a most unwelcome sight for a weary homeward-bound mariner. One old-time skipper who defied the signal made a reckless dash for the entrance, when a huge sea lifted his smack and carried it *over* the outer pier, dumping him squarely in the harbour! Known as Mad Isaac, his name lived on long after him with local people using the expression "you Mad Isaac!" whenever they thought someone was being foolish!

Sadly, we have no way of knowing today just who Mad Isaac was, but there was a well-known smack owner called Isaac Cox at Scarborough in the 1880s and '90s. Could he have been the one?

"Brandy for the Parson, 'Baccy for the Clerk"

The *Newcastle Courant* of September 5th, 1778 reported

> "Tuesday 25th ult. Smuggling cutter aground Redcar Rocks. Total loss. Another smuggling cutter came to assist, and removed goods, tea, spirits etc. Fine seizures might have been made by the commanders of the king's cruizers had they been attentive to their duty."

Another smuggling vessel got stranded here at Redcar on February 28th, 1822. On this occasion it was local fishermen who assisted the casualty off the rocks. They were rewarded for their efforts in contraband gin!

Gin from Holland was a favoured cargo amongst smugglers; Thomas Dent, one such smuggler, established a ferry service across the Humber as a "sideline" in 1803. The landing place on the Lincolnshire side is still known to this day as New Holland because of the amount of contraband Dutch gin which Dent landed there.

In the year 1798, at the suggestion of Captain Sir Hugh Popham RN, the Royal Navy established the Sea Fencibles – an armed defence unit, set up in response to the threat of French invasion. Chosen from "watermen" associated with the coast, they were trained in gunnery and were given freedom from the press-gangs whose role was to kidnap unwary mariners and drag them off to serve in the King's Navy. The Fencibles were equipped with small boats and were used in the constant

war against privateers and smugglers.

The Redcar Sea Fencibles, commanded by Captain Thrush, were called to arms shortly after midnight on March 8th, 1804, when gunfire was heard at sea. It transpired that the guns were not a threat but a distress call. The brig *Rose* of London, from Christiansand with timber, had run onto Redcar Rocks. The vessel became a total wreck but, happily, the 26 crew were saved by local fishermen.

After the Battle of Trafalgar, the threat of foreign invasion virtually disappeared and the Sea Fencibles were disbanded. Their part in the war against smugglers had not been significant – in truth smuggling during the period had become such a major industry that virtually the whole populations of villages like Staithes and Robin Hood's Bay were involved in it to some extent. Smuggling was not regarded as a real crime by most villagers and the Customs and Excise men were generally vilified.

A new revenue force called the Preventative Waterguard was set up in 1809, and the London to Berwick area (district 3) was equipped with 4 cruisers and 13 smaller boats. The organisation changed again in 1821, when it became the Coastguard, a partly naval and partly civilian force. The revenue cruisers were taken out of Customs' control in 1816, from which time they came under the control of the Admiralty. These bureaucratic changes were to have little effect on the smuggling trade, however, though it did eventually change because of the economic climate.

Pulling the Wool Over the Customs' Eyes

It is well known that in life there are only two unavoidable things: one is death and the other, taxes. The taxes on imports and exports, normally known by the more user-friendly name of "duties", are much older than one might imagine. The first written record of taxation on goods imported into the country dates back to the year 742, and we have King Aethelbad of Mercia to thank for it.

Almost as old as taxes are the attempts to make money by circumventing them – an occupation that we have come to know as smuggling, and the Yorkshire coast was no stranger to this way of life.

Strangely, perhaps, the earliest form of smuggling here was the outward smuggling of wool, beginning in the fourteenth century. The reason for this particular duty was that the king wanted the wool to be woven into cloth in this country. It was a laudable attempt to encourage the weaving trade here, rather than in Flanders where weavers were well established. The duty raised by wool exports was colossal, averaging about £10,000 per annum in the 1350s, an indication of just how much wool was being legally exported.

Prominent in the wool export trade were the religious orders of the day and some monasteries conducted thriving businesses buying wool from farmers, even though such trade was banned by their order. They were not above a little smuggling either. In 1276 Peter the Black of Scarborough was caught shipping 70 sacks of "uncustomed" wool out through the port of Filey, price nine marks per sack, and, at the same time, the Prior of Bridlington had shipped 60 sacks through Filey without having paid duty.

Smugglers would go to great lengths to conceal their actions. In 1367 a ship bound for Flanders was wrecked on Filey Brigg, coal laden – or so it seemed. Underneath a layer of coal in her hold were wool bales on which no duty had been paid. They must have been trying to pull the wool over the customs men's eyes!

Henry Freeman, Lifeboat Hero

Henry Freeman was a most remarkable man and, although he died in 1904, he is still remembered with great pride in his adopted home of Whitby. Born in 1836, he lived much of his early life at Bridlington where he worked as a bricklayer and tile-maker until, at the age of twenty, he moved to Whitby to answer the call of the sea. He made a few coastal voyages as a seaman on the London run and then turned his hand to fishing.

It was during the great storm of February 9th, 1861 that Freeman was to come into prominence. On that morning, along with six other fishermen, he was to be found walking along the seashore at Whitby, looking to see what useful items might have been cast ashore. They saw the Sunderland brig *John and Ann* in distress off Sandsend a little north of the town and, realising that she was about to take the ground and inevitably break up, they launched a coble and went to the rescue. Of the seven rescuers, Freeman was the only one who was not part of the local lifeboat crew. Their mission was successful: the five crew of the brig were landed safely. By 10 o'clock, the rescuers were back in Whitby where they assembled at the lifeboat house, ready to carry out further rescues that they knew would be needed. They didn't have to wait long: the schooner *Gamma*, laden with coals for London, ran aground close to the piers. But, the lifeboat was ready and the four crew were taken off without incident.

Freeman and his new colleagues stood by. Though cold and wet they fortified themselves with grog – rum and water – the seaman's tonic and, before long, went to the rescue of the crew of the Sunderland barque *Clara*. This time it was more difficult; being larger, the barque had stranded further offshore and, with the eleven crew having taken to the rigging, the job of saving them called for great skill and courage by the rescuers. Nevertheless, the rescue was accomplished; minutes afterwards the *Clara* capsized and started to break up. John Storr, lifeboat coxswain, and his eleven crew were afforded another short break – when the harbourmaster warned them against going for a drink, as there would be more work for them that day. And so there was. The brig *Utility* and the schooner *Roe* came ashore within minutes of each other and, in both cases, the crews were rescued by Storr and his men. At about two o'clock that same day two more ships were seen approaching in distress. The *Flora,* a London schooner, made it through the piers before running ashore, but in a safe place. The *Merchant,* another schooner from Maldon, attempted to follow suit but missed the entrance and stranded forty yards outside the pier. By now the seas were terrible to behold, but the lifeboat was soon manned by the same crew, plus an extra man, making thirteen in all. They succeeded in getting out to the stricken vessel, after a Herculean struggle.

It was at this point that things went horribly wrong. A combination of cross seas threw up a freak wave which lifted the lifeboat high out of the water and turned her over, throwing the crew into a raging sea. Henry Freeman, who had worn a patent cork lifebelt throughout the day, was the only survivor.

An inquest into the events of that day was held later, and much of it centred around whether or not the lifeboat crew had consumed more grog than was good for them between their rescue missions. It seems a little harsh to suggest that those brave men might have been less than fully sober; and in any case it was irrelevant. Any seaman knows that from time to time a sea will come along which is more than any small boat can deal with, whether the crew is roaring drunk or stone-cold sober.

Henry Freeman was awarded the Silver Medal of the RNLI for his heroism that day. He went on to become the coxswain of the Whitby lifeboat, and rightly so. In one day he had seen more action than many seamen see in a lifetime, and he went on to see very much more.

He was no angel, however. He had a number of disputes with the RNLI over the years, and he made enemies amongst his crews. Worse still, perhaps, in April 1883 he and three others were found guilty of stealing three fishing lines at sea. At the time he was skipper of the fishing boat *Alexandria* and his lines had become entangled with those of another fisherman, the defence argued. Freeman had found it necessary to cut the other man's lines, but had then taken them ashore and kept them. His colleagues were fined £5 each; Freeman, as skipper, was fined £15, a considerable sum at that time.

One of the most famous lifeboat rescues along the Yorkshire coast was that which took place on January 19th, 1881, when the 58-year-old brig *Visitor* was wrecked in Robin Hood's Bay. The local vicar, Reverend J. Cooper, alerted Whitby Lifeboat station and received the reply:

"Leaving with the lifeboat at once – send men and horses to meet us."

The Whitby lifeboat was brought the eight miles by road, through thick snowdrifts, in very difficult circumstances. Sixty men preceded the boat hacking a way through the snow for the 200 men and eleven horses that were pulling the lifeboat. Against all the odds, the lifeboat was launched and on its second attempt saved all the crew of the wrecked ship. It was a truly remarkable act of heroism, by a lot of men, with Henry Freeman prominent amongst them.

There were many other notable rescues led by this giant of a man over the next eighteen years, and he became deservedly famous, featuring in one of Frank Meadow Sutcliffe's best-known photographs. He won a second Silver Medal, and finally retired on a pension at the age of 63, in 1899.

Henry Freeman had been a lifeboatman for 38 years and had assisted in the saving of over 300 lives. At the age of 68 he died, appropriately perhaps, at the height of a north-easterly gale.

The Changing Fortunes of George Jolliffe

George Jolliffe was a Filey fisherman, owner of a five-man yawl named the *Fair Susan,* his pride and joy. He was fishing for cod on the Dogger Bank when, on November 5th, 1821, the strong north-easterly wind increased to gale and then storm force. It was a dark, scowling morning and many fishing boats and colliers in the area turned to run for Scarborough or Filey Bay. By noon the seas were running mountains high and the screaming wind reached hurricane force.

To the nor'ard, thirty vessels were driven ashore near Redcar, and at least fifteen others were wrecked elsewhere on the Yorkshire coast. George did not know of these disasters, though his own years of experience told him that not all would reach safety that day.

Eventually, the *Fair Susan* reached the safety of Filey Bay and George and his crew anchored and landed in their small boat, exhausted, but glad to be alive.

Later that day, a merchant vessel under bare poles was seen to be driving helplessly towards Speeton Cliffs, at the south end of Filey Bay. Distress guns were being fired from the ship as rescuers hurried along the cliffs in the gathering darkness. The ship had already lost one of her masts; men could be seen on the deck, and the watchers shuddered as they saw seas sweeping over the vessel as she took the ground. A white-haired old man could be seen lashed to the mainmast, as the battered hull seemed to dissolve in the liquid chaos.Ropes thrown from the cliffs by the would-be rescuers were blown back by the wind and the crowd watched helplessly as wreckage was thrown in all directions.

Next morning the wind had abated considerably, and George set off with others to look for the old man, whose image had kept him awake all night. They found his body, still tied to the broken mast, and discovered an address in Hull in the man's pocket. George travelled to Hull to deliver the old man's body to his family, named Anckersvoerd, and a funeral was arranged.

Before that winter was out, the *Fair Susan* herself was wrecked, leaving George Jolliffe penniless. Word reached the Anckersvoerd family and the son turned up in Filey – to buy George the best fishing smack that money could buy, worth, at that time, £100, in gratitude for the concern he had shown for the fate of the white-haired old man.

Paddling Down to London

It had taken many hundreds of years to bring the sailing ship to the degree of perfection it had achieved by the late nineteenth century, so it is little wonder that the steamship, when it arrived, was not an overnight success. In truth, however, it took only a few decades to convince shipowners that the birth of the steamboat did effectively mark the demise of sail for all practical purposes.

As early as the year 1736, a patent had been taken out by one Jonathon Hulls for a design for a paddle-driven steamer to be powered by a Newcomen "atmospheric" engine; but, at that time, the technology required to build the vessel did not exist. Many scientists and engineers worked on the problem in the ensuing decades, but it was not until 1775 that a steamboat ran on the Seine. Twenty-six years later, in 1801, the *Charlotte Dundas* was launched on the Clyde, and she was used to replace horses in towing barges on canals. Although she succeeded in this, she was withdrawn from service because of the damage to the canal banks that her paddles caused. In 1812, the paddle steamer *Comet* was launched on the Clyde as a passenger vessel, and she made history by becoming the first commercial steamer to operate in the world.

In August 1822, a fleet of ships carrying King George IV sailed up the east coast bound for the Scottish capital and when it returned, later in the month, the fleet was accompanied by two paddle steamers. These may well have been the first steamships to sail along the Yorkshire coast; certainly the fleet created enormous excitement among the people of Scarborough, who turned out in force to watch them pass by.

It was a year after this, in 1823, that the first passenger steamship service was established along the east coast: the steamer *Tourist* ran from Edinburgh to London, calling at Whitby to pick up passengers once a week. She was just the first of many, and it is easy to understand why. The journey from London to Newcastle by stagecoach cost £4.50 (or £2.25 outside), and was uncomfortable and time-consuming. The steamer fare was £2.00, including food and accommodation. Consequently, the coastal steamer trade thrived and brought with it a whole host of fascinating tales, none more entertaining than that of the *Caledonia*.

Built in 1836 at Blackwall on the Thames, *Caledonia* was a 721-ton paddle steamer built for the General Steam Navigation Company of Leith and London. She was 172 feet long, had 200 nominal horsepower engines, and a reputation for being particularly fast.

In the early part of her career the *Caledonia* worked the London to Hamburg run under Captain G. Sellers; but not all her activities were above board. She made the news in 1842 when her great speed failed her, and she was caught smuggling!

Later, she was put on the Leith (Edinburgh) to London run, and became familiar with the Yorkshire Coast – too familiar, for on 29 February, 1864 she ended her days here.

Like many other ships before and after her, the *Caledonia* got "out of her reckoning" during a dense fog and struck rocks at Flamborough Head. Because of her shallow draught, she had got herself into very shallow water when she struck and this made it easier for the passengers and crew to scramble ashore. The ship quickly broke up, however, and it was not long before her cargo began to wash up on the beach. The local populace were not slow in noticing this, and large crowds of beachcombers assembled to gather what they could.

The *Scarborough Gazette* of March 10th, 1864 reported that the beach had been strewn with merchandise, including " … jewellery, beautiful trinkets, and casks of porter … "

The police and coastguards were much in evidence in an attempt to prevent the looters from leaving the beach with their ill-gotten gains. They did manage to secure a good quantity which would be returned to its rightful owners, but they were outwitted by one lady who appeared to be " … in a delicate state … ", i.e. heavily pregnant. The officials were far too gentlemanly to challenge her; as a result she was able to stagger up the cliffs bearing a considerable amount of loot!

The Ship That Came Home to Die

On Saturday September 10th, 1881 the South Shields shipbuilding company of John Readhead & Co. launched from its West Dock a fine new steamer called *Wydale*. She was one of the few ocean-going steamships ever to be registered and owned at Scarborough, and had been built to the order of one Pantland Hick, a well-known local shipowner and one-time Mayor of Scarborough.

The *Wydale* was an iron schooner-rigged steamship of 1981 tons, powered by 185-horsepower compound engines. She also carried sails, for mariners were still not entirely convinced of the reliability of steam engines at this time. She was 275-feet long, could carry 2,500 tons of cargo at a speed of nine knots, and was designed for the Atlantic trade – she was far too big ever to enter her home port of Scarborough.

Great excitement accompanied the launching ceremony, and more than 100 guests assembled to watch Mr Hick send the ship down the launching ways. Among the guests, Mr B.W. Hick had more reason than most to feel proud, for he was to be captain of the splendid vessel.

The *Wydale* carried Lloyd's highest insurance rating of 100 AI, and seemed all set to conquer the world's oceans. Who would have guessed on that day that she was due to end her life less than twenty years hence, on the rocks just a few miles from Scarborough?

She was first registered at Scarborough on October 20th, 1881 and, within a month, Pantland Hick had sold shares in the vessel to people as far afield as Manchester, Rochdale and Lytham; there was no shortage of people waiting to put their money into so fine a ship.

For more than two years *Wydale* plied the oceans without incident, until on December 18th, 1884 tragedy came her way. She was bound for Cardiff, in ballast from Le Havre, when, off Prawle Point in Devon, she ran down a small sailing vessel called *Band of Hope*. The hapless sailing boat was also heading west, but was unable to make much progress because of light winds when *Wydale* bore down on her at full speed and cut her to the waterline, sinking her instantly. By the time the steamer had slowed down and turned round, it was too late; no trace was found of the two crew of the *Band of Hope*. The subsequent Board of Trade inquiry found that the steamer was at fault; she had been travelling at speed without a proper lookout. The captain was held responsible, and his certificate was suspended for three months.

A second incident in the career of the *Wydale* had a happier note. In July of 1887 she was instrumental in saving the whole crew of a large American ship called the *Baymore*, which had struck a semi-submerged wreck, and as a result, was in a sinking condition herself. The crew of the schooner had been lashed to the port quarter to prevent themselves being washed overboard, and had been thus, without food or water, for two days when the *Wydale* came to their rescue. The steamer was en route for Rouen from New Orleans at the time of the incident.

For ten more years, the *Wydale* traded between ports all over the western world, until October 2nd, 1897 when Pantland Hick bought back all the shares in the vessel. Two weeks later, he sold the ship to Matthew Lowden of Glasgow, but she retained her Scarborough registration.

Her new owners were soon to have problems with *Wydale*. In November, 1899 she arrived in Prince's Dock, Glasgow, with her cargo of esparto grass on fire. So serious was the problem that the ship was purposely submerged for three days in order to douse the flames; but when she was raised again, the fire broke out again. Eventually, it was put out, but £5,000 worth of cargo was lost, and the damage to the ship cost even more.

Not long after this the ship was sold to the Compania La Blanca, Bilbao, Spain, and was registered anew in that country. Now sailing as the *San Antonio,* the nineteen-year-old steamer left Bilbao in December 1900 under a new master, Captain V. Berojam, with 2,600 tons of iron ore for Newcastle – but the ore was never delivered.

On Monday, December 10th, 1900 the *San Antonio* ran ashore 400 yards south of Long Nab, Burniston, within sight of her old home port. Though the passengers were saved, the ship was doomed; she had stranded across a reef of rocks known as the Horseback, and there was to be no escape. The following day the 23 crew left the *San Antonio* and, shortly afterwards, she broke her back and sank.

Today her remains lie rusting beneath the waves, almost – but not quite – forgotten. Local divers occasionally swim over her bones, and local anglers still call the place where she lies *San Antonio.*

Sharp-Eyed Bill and the Dan-Buoy

Bill Sheader, known to his friends as "Jitter", was a highly-respected fisherman, as well as a decorated coxswain of the Scarborough Lifeboat, a position he held for many years. Bill ran a fishing coble from Scarborough, together with another fisherman who was known, for obvious reasons, as Filey Bill. They formed a hardworking and successful partnership, routinely going off to sea in the wee small hours, and returning around lunchtime, hopefully with a good catch of fish or, more often, lobsters and crabs. They had a number of favourite spots for shooting their fleets of lobster pots, usually 30 pots to a fleet, with each end marked by a dan-buoy. Each of the local fishermen would have his own colour code or shape of buoy to distinguish his pots from those of his colleagues and rivals. The cobles would usually fish within 10 or 15 miles of their home port, and it was always a bone of contention between Bill and Filey Bill as to who would be the first to spot their tell-tale buoys as they steamed towards them. It is worth pointing out that they carried no sophisticated electronics for position finding; navigation was done by the Mark One Eyeball on Bill's coble. One day, Filey Bill's self-proclaimed superior eyesight drove Bill to seek revenge. After the day's work was done, Bill went back to sea on his own, without Filey Bill's knowledge. He steamed straight out to sea for a distance of ten miles, then threw overboard an anchor and cable to which he attached a specially prepared dan-buoy: a red float with a white stick and a green flag. He then steamed home.

Next morning, as the coble left Scarborough, Bill asked casually "What's that dan yonder?" pointing seawards. Filey Bill could, of course, see nothing. Bill turned the coble in the direction he had indicated, and after a few minutes said "Look – it's a green flag – surely tha' can see it!" Filey Bill peered fruitlessly. Five more minutes passed, and Bill chimed in again "Aye – it's a green flag on a white stick." No response from Filey Bill. When the coble was within a mile of where Bill knew the dan to be, he dealt the final blow. "Surely you can see that. A green flag on a white stick on a red float. It sticks out a mile!" Minutes later, poor Filey Bill finally spotted the bait. "Oh aye, I've got it now – but I can't make out the colours" (Bill, incidentally, could see no trace of the bouy at this time. He just knew where it was.)

As Filey Bill slowly started to be able to distinguish the colours, he turned to his old pal and admitted, "I'm damned if I know how you spotted that when you did." Jitter smiled inwardly, well pleased with his harmless ploy.

The Hawkwood Mystery

There can be few people who have not heard of the mystery of the ill-fated *Marie Celeste,* yet the circumstances surrounding the loss of the *Hawkwood* are almost unknown, even though they are probably even stranger. Odder yet is the fact that this disaster took place ashore, at the south end of Filey Bay, and still within living memory.

The *Hawkwood* was a London-based collier steamship of some 1155 tons, built in 1899, and valued at £14,000 at the time of her loss. She was bound for London with a cargo of coal from Granton in the Firth of Forth, in January of 1913, when a south-east gale sprang up. She was seen by the Newcastle steamer *Newark* at 8.30am on the 12th of January, two miles off Flamborough Head, with a list to port and, though all her lights were blazing, she seemed deserted. It was evident that her starboard lifeboat had been launched. A siren blast from the *Newark* brought no response, and there was no sign of life aboard. The captain of the *Newark* was concerned: *Hawkwood* and her crew were well known to the men of the collier fleet, and the weather was appalling at sea that day.

As the weather drove the stricken ship towards the rocks, she was observed by people ashore. A crowd gathered to witness her final destruction as she grounded close to King and Queen Rocks, under Speeton Cliffs. They watched in horror as the 235-foot ship capsized and started to break up, spewing her cargo onto the beach.

No trace was ever found of Captain Hibbert or the seventeen crew.

It transpired later that the ship had a design fault: the fuel bunker space at one side of the ship was much greater than at the other, because of an offset donkey boiler. This meant that the trim of the ship was continually having to be altered as the fuel was burned, otherwise a list was inevitable. On this occasion, the list must have become so great that the crew thought they were about to sink. Sadly, had they remained aboard, they might well have survived, for when the tide ebbed, *Hawkwood* was left high and dry, with little water inside the wreck.

There is a postscript to this story. *Hawkwood II* was built for the same company in 1934, at a cost of £38,750. She was bigger than her namesake at 2,024 tons, but strangely was to suffer a similar fate. In January, 1942 she sailed late from the Tees trying to join up with a southbound convoy and by Whitby she had almost caught up. However, the convoy's escort ship could not wait and ordered *Hawkwood II* back to the Tees to await the next convoy. She obeyed and anchored off Tees Bay until the wind went round to the north-east and she was obliged to move. In raising her anchor, *Hawkwood II* fouled her propellor on a rope from a boom defence across the river mouth and she drove ashore, where she broke up. Happily, on this occasion, the crew were saved, being rescued by breeches-buoy from the shore.

The Arrival of the Sinful Steamboat!

In the early part of the nineteenth century steamboats began to appear around Britain's coastline. They were seen in Yorkshire ports by around 1820. At first, there was some uncertainty as to what this newfangled invention was actually going to be used for, and there was a lot of distrust among the hardened sailors of the day, who put their faith in sail and oar, as their forefathers had done. There was one obvious use to which they could be put, however, and that was to tow the *real* ships in and out of port when the wind would not allow them to use their sails. As a consequence of this, every port and harbour in the country soon had its own fleet of steam tugs for this purpose, most of them paddle driven, because such vessels were highly manoeuvrable and were shallow drafted. Over the next few decades, however, sail gradually gave

way to steam, and many paddle tugs found themselves redundant for the new breed of steamships did not need tugs to get them out to sea.

It did not take enterprising steam-tug owners long to realise that they could earn an honest shilling by running excursions for tourists from the popular spa towns and holiday resorts of the Yorkshire coast.

The earliest of these vessels at Scarborough was the *Royal Victoria,* described as the largest and most powerful steamer on the Tees, from where she hailed. Each summer from 1847 on, she visited Scarborough in the summer months, bringing day trippers from Hartlepool, each of whom had paid four shillings. The steamer was commanded by Captain Cass, one of the three owners of the ship, who was described in the company literature as being " ... steady, attentive and *sober*." It might seem strange that it was thought necessary to mention this third virtue – but as further stories will show, this could not be taken for granted among captains of the day!

Right from the start, there seemed to be something "not quite nice" about steamboat rides, at least in the eyes of some, as this next tale indicates.

In August of 1849, Mr Pickup, landlord of the "Queen's Head" in Scarborough, chartered the Hartlepool steamer *Firebrand* to run two day trips, and he quickly sold 150 tickets to the eager public. To his great embarrassment the steamer failed to arrive on the appointed day, and the ticket-holders were left standing on the quay in a state of great indignation. On the second day the steamer *again* failed to appear and Mr Pickup was left with an even redder face.

Some time later, Mr Pickup received a letter from the owner of *Firebrand* explaining that he had decided not to honour the agreement because he had become firmly convinced that such excursions led to " ... nothing but sin and drunkenness, and would produce nothing but sorrow and misery at last ... "

Coals from Newcastle

Most of the shipping that passed up and down the Yorkshire coast over the centuries was involved in the coal trade from the north-east coal-fields to London and beyond. No one can now be certain just when this trade began, but there are records to show that "sea cole" from Newcastle was in use in London as early as 1299. By the late 1300s, there was a regular trade with thousands of tons of coal leaving the Tyne each year, much of it bound for what we now know as Holland and Belgium. In these early years, coal was used mainly by smiths. It was not until the sixteenth century that it became widely used as a domestic fuel, by which time there was a desperate shortage of timber in England. In any case, shipbuilding had become a national priority as a result of wars and foreign trade, and what was left of England's great forests assumed a new importance.

By the year 1776, the number of ships carrying coal had increased to the extent that the economist Adam Smith said that the trade employed " … more ships than all the carrying trade of England … " The coal trade was sometimes referred to as the "nursery of the navy", for many seamen learned their skills aboard coal ships – including no less a person than the famous Captain Cook of Whitby. When Cook sailed on his historic voyages of discovery, he chose to use Whitby-built colliers rather than Royal Navy ships, to the horror of the Lords of the Admiralty. He knew that such vessels, being strongly built and flat-bottomed, were suitable for exploring unknown coasts, where they might have to be beached for repairs, using local materials, and their own shipwrights' skills. This did indeed happen during Cook's voyages, and it did much to enhance the reputation of the Whitby-built ships.

During the late 1700s, most colliers were three-masted vessels of about 300 tons, and were known as "cats" – indeed it is thought that Dick Whittington made his fortune with one of these; his cat was probably a coal-carrying ship, not an animal of the feline species!

During these early years, coal-carrying ships were not generally owned in Newcastle and London, but rather in Scarborough and Whitby – possibly because the local shipowners were more aware of the potential profits, and had suitable vessels. Both ports earned a reputation for building colliers, which, once launched and put into the coal trade, never saw their home port again!

The Yorkshire ports of Whitby, Scarborough and Bridlington benefitted in yet another way from the coal trade, for these ports were, above all, "harbours of refuge" – places where any ship could seek shelter in time of storm. Because the vast majority of passing ships were in fact colliers, it was thought fit that they should pay for the privilege of having such harbours at their disposal. Accordingly, a system of "passing tolls" was introduced, whereby every passing collier was required to pay a toll, whether they used the harbours or not. The idea was that this money would be used to keep the ports of refuge in a good state of repair.

By the year 1800, most colliers were two-masted vessels called brigs, a type that was nimble, strong, and easily handled by a small crew. They were crewed by five men and a boy, with the captain more often than not owning shares in the vessel. All of them lived uncomfortably for the four-day voyage: the mate would usually share the captain's cabin aft, while the other five would sleep in the fo'c'sle, where there was no standing headroom, and all manner of evil-smelling ship's gear was stored. The food was generally poor: salt beef and biscuits in meagre portions – it was in the captain's own interest to keep costs down. And all this was the good news!

The bad news was that collier brigs over the ensuing years earned the reputation of being the lowest form of craft afloat, simply because their owners, in the search for profit, kept them at sea for years after they were fit only for firewood. Worse still, they were often grossly over-loaded, and then insured for large sums. The owner would benefit whether the ship reached its destination or not, and there were many cases when it seemed clear that the owners would be quite satisfied for the heavily-insured vessel to sink. They became known to seamen as "coffin ships".

The number of coal-carrying ships that sank off the Yorkshire coast over the years is truly astounding; no complete record of these losses exists, but odd bits of information have filtered through. We know, for instance, that in November of 1696, 200 colliers were wrecked on the east coast in a single storm. In January of 1800, 71 colliers left the coal ports for London, and 69 of them were lost. Similarly, in January of 1857, 76 colliers were wrecked between Flamborough Head and the Tyne, with the loss of more than 100 lives. Board of Trade figures for the year 1865 show that no less than 675 collier brigs were lost in the year, all due to stress of weather, sometimes made worse by unseaworthy ships.

For the sailors that survived these disasters, there was another sting in the tail. If the ship did not reach its destination, the crew would receive no wages, even if they had been at sea for days, weeks, months, or even years.

The "*Star of the West*" was a 202-ton brigantine – as opposed to a brig, which was rigged differently – that had been built in 1869 for the West Indian and South American trades, where she served out most of her useful life. Instead of being scrapped, she was put into the coal trade, and on March 30th, 1892 left the Tyne with 348 tons of coal – and five inches of water in her hold. Bound for Jersey, she had eight crew, including Captain Saunders. The water level in the hold began to rise as the vessel headed south. As they neared Scarborough the level rose to eleven and then fifteen feet, despite the fact that all hands were manning the pumps. It became clear that she was doomed, and the ship's boat was launched into a flat calm sea at 6am on 31 March. The crew waited alongside until the old ship settled, bow first, beneath the sea. The Scarborough paddle-trawler *Lord Clyde* saw the whole thing taking place and rescued the crew, landing them at Scarborough. *Star of the West* was valued at around £650 and was insured. The owners would suffer no loss; only the crew would lose out. Had the weather not been so kind that day, they might well have lost more than just their wages.

The Intrepid Yachtsmen

It was Ratty in *Wind in the Willows* who first observed that there is simply *nothing* half as well worth doing as "messing about in boats". Generations of Englishmen and women have agreed wholeheartedly, and when one Bridlington couple were offered the opportunity of borrowing a small sailing boat, which we will call for the sake of argument the *Saucy Sue*, they jumped at the chance. Sensibly, they obtained appropriate clothing and safety equipment and, even better, they bought a book called *All You Need to Know About Sailing*, which they read avidly.

By the time they felt ready to embark on their maiden voyage, there was little they didn't know about halyards, sheets, shrouds and

39

stays. They even knew about futtocks, ramplanks, gunwhales and goosenecks; and soundings, shoals and cardinal marks held no mystery for our well-read, would-be mariners.

Even so, when they put to sea early one Sunday morning on a fine summer's day, they were cautious about straying too far from the harbour mouth. Before long they had the little vessel broad-reaching, running by the lee, tacking and gybing like Americas Cup winners. But sailing is quite strenuous and is known to sharpen the appetite. So, after a couple of hours, the crew of the *Saucy Sue* felt in need of sustenance, as well as a well-earned rest. They didn't want to go back into the harbour and were reluctant to deploy the anchor as that would entail more back-aching effort. So, instead, they moored up to one of a pair of large orange buoys, conveniently placed a little way out from the harbour mouth.

Before long they had a veritable feast spread out before them in the boat's cockpit and, as they started to eat, noticed that a whole lot of other yachts were coming out of the harbour, to-ing and fro-ing, and getting ever nearer to the moored picnickers.

"What friendly people yachties are!" our heroes exclaimed. "Look how they are all waving and shouting to us!"

As the approaching fleet came ever nearer a loud report came from the pier, and the waving and shouting became louder. Our intrepid mariners were puzzled, and becoming a little alarmed. The nearest of the approaching yachts, now shouting very loudly indeed, was only feet away, when a second loud report was heard, and our picnicking pair suddenly saw the light. They realised to their horror that a Royal Yorkshire Yacht Club race had just started and that the *Saucy Sue* was tied to the windward start mark. The little yacht was lying, fair and square, across the start line of the race!

"Perhaps it might have been wise to have read the chapter on yacht-racing after all," the pair mused later.

The Scarborough Minefield

During World War I, nothing outraged the people of Yorkshire more than the bombardment of Scarborough by a fleet of German ships in December 1914. Nineteen people were killed and a further eighty were injured. The cry "Remember Scarborough!" was used in recruitment posters, so great was the anger felt.

What was not clear at the time was that the bombardment was nothing more than a cover for an even greater threat. While the German battle-cruisers *Derfflinger* and *Von Der Tann* were firing their shells at the town, the light cruiser *Kolberg* was engaged in laying, what proved to be, the densest minefield ever known in the history of naval warfare just off the Scarborough coast.

There is a theory that the intention of the German ships was to try and lure the British Grand Fleet into this minefield, and there are strong arguments for this. But whether or not this was the case, the minefield did have devastating results, many of which did not become apparent until the last few years. Many ships in the war years simply disappeared without trace: they left their home ports and failed to reach their destinations. At the time, many of these unfortunate vessels were listed as "lost in the North Sea". Discoveries by amateur divers of Scarborough Sub-Aqua Club in recent years have shown that many such losses were, in fact, victims of the *Kolberg's* mines. The toll currently stands at twenty ships; there may well be more.

The first victims succumbed almost before the raiders were out of sight: the 1190-ton Norwegian collier *Vaaren* struck a mine between Filey and Scarborough, and she was quickly followed by the 1228-ton

Elterwater, another collier, and the 988-ton *Princess Olga*, carrying a general cargo. On this first day, December 16th, there was no indication as to the extent or density of the minefield, but when a group of minesweeping trawlers from Grimsby steamed in on December 19, they were soon to find out.

It was a brilliantly-clear morning as the trawlers steamed past Filey, blackening the sky with their smoke, their sweeps out in readiness. Within the first five minutes they had exploded eighteen mines, and as they got into the thick of the field the falling tide brought the anchored mines closer to the surface. Each had five horns, and contained some 350lbs of explosive.

At 11am, the 273-ton minesweeping trawler *Orianda* struck a mine while steaming full ahead, and her momentum caused her to plough herself under the waves, her masthead cutting through the water like a submarine's periscope as she sank. Surprisingly, only one man was lost; Lt. H. B. Boothby and the rest of his crew were picked up from the water very quickly. A second trawler, the *Passing*, was also mined and a huge hole was blown in her bows; but she did not sink, and was eventually beached at Scarborough for repairs. Significantly, perhaps, she was new and was the biggest trawler in the country at the time.

The sweepers found themselves in a desperate situation by this time as the full horror of the minefield became apparent. As the tide fell, they were in the midst of a horrible mêlée of floating mines, tangled wire sweeps and stricken trawlers, all drifting with the current. Operations were suspended until the tide rose again. The next day, the 203-ton auxiliary patrol trawler *Garmo* was blown up and sunk with the loss of six lives, including that of the skipper, T. Gilbert.

The loss of merchant ships continued: the 1168-ton *Boston* was crippled by a mine, but drifted onto Filey Brigg before sinking, and Christmas Day saw the loss of no less than four ships. The 464-ton *Gem* was blown in half with the loss of ten men; *Therese Heymann*, 2393-tons, was lost with all hands off Filey; the minesweeper *Nighthawk* blew up with the loss of six lives, and the 1107-ton *Eli* sank off Cayton Bay without loss of life. Boxing Day brought three more victims, and the last day of 1914 brought another: the 2458-ton Danish steamer *M. C. Holm* that had been posted as "lost in the North Sea" until Scarborough divers found and identified her recently.

A fourth minesweeping trawler fell victim to the Scarborough minefield on January 6th, 1915, when the 480-ton *Banyers* struck a mine and sank, taking six men's lives. The skipper escaped by scrambling out through the wheelhouse window as the trawler took its final plunge – he was no less a man than Lt. H. B. Boothby, who, it will be remembered, had already had one trawler, the *Orianda*, blown up from under him! Boothby was awarded the DSO – as he put it himself, for losing two ships!

It was many months before the last of the 100 mines had either done its deadly work, or been cleared, and hundreds of men died as a result. We shall probably never know the full extent of the damage and death that was caused by the Scarborough Minefield.

The Merry Master of the Mary Ellen

Of all the pleasure-steamer stories, my own particular favourite is that of the *Mary Ellen,* a Glasgow-built vessel that was registered in Lancaster, but ran trips from Scarborough. On June 6th, 1897, her first trip of the season, she sailed from her home port in thick fog, carrying almost a hundred passengers. Two miles south of the harbour she struck rocks in Cayton Bay and started taking water. Pandemonium ensued on board and the cries of the passengers attracted the attention of a passing steam trawler, the *Patriot*, which sent a small boat over to offer assistance in getting the passengers off the stranded vessel. Captain Rees Evans of the *Mary Ellen* refused the offer, however – he was afraid that passengers might panic and overload the small boat, with disastrous results. Having made this decision, he then fainted! This did not inspire the passengers with confidence!

After a while, Rees Evans came round to find the mate, Charles Kemp, at the wheel steering a course for Scarborough, the vessel having refloated on the rising tide. The captain – who was also the owner of the vessel – was not happy with this situation, and tried to wrest the wheel from Kemp's grasp. Members of the crew took Kemp's side in the struggle, and as the steamer approached Scarborough harbour, watchers on the pier were treated to the sight of the vessel materialising out of the fog with much shouting and screaming, and a full-scale battle taking place on the bridge! As the ship came alongside the pier, harbour staff jumped aboard in order to moor her up, while the distraught passengers disembarked in a mad scramble, some of them jumping into small cobles that were nearby, others leaping for the pier

before the gangplank was deployed. It was clear to all concerned that the captain was seriously drunk!

At the ensuing Board of Trade inquiry, it transpired that the vessel was not overloaded, carried all the required safety equipment, and had a full complement of crew – five in number. The mate stated that on the outbound trip, Rees Evans had ordered him to steer SSE, a course he knew to be wrong, but the captain's word is law at sea. Fifteen minutes later, Evans took the wheel himself, and soon after a deckhand shouted "Breakers ahead", and the ship ran hard aground.

The court found that Evans had been wrong in going to sea in the prevailing fog; that he had been under the influence of drink, and that the vessel was not navigated properly. His certificate was suspended for two years. The rest of the officers and crew were exonerated of all blame.

Within a month of the inquiry, the *Mary Ellen* was put up for auction. She failed to make her reserve price, was withdrawn, and left

Scarborough under a cloud shortly afterwards.

There is a postscript to this story, however. A year later, the *Mary Ellen* reappeared at Scarborough with a new owner, Mr J. Burns, and a new name – she was now the *Larmont* of West Hartlepool. She continued to ply her trade for at least two more years, without further serious incidents!

The True Abstainer

More than one of the tales in this little collection has made reference to the fact that many seamen through the ages have been partial to the odd alcoholic beverage, and there have been extreme cases where this has led to real problems with dire consequences.

Because of this, there has long been a fight against alcohol, led by the Temperance Society which organised weekly meetings in many fishing ports. At one such meeting, held in Scarborough on Monday, October 29th, 1850 in the George Street Chapel, those present were addressed by (among others) the young skipper of the Yarmouth smack *Gypsey Queen*.

Described by the local newspaper reporter as a man with eleven years' experience as a teetotaller, the young skipper told how all his crew were teetotal, as were the entire crew of his father's vessel, the *True Abstainer.* Both vessels sailed under the Bethel Flag and regularly held temperance meetings while out on the German Ocean (what we now call the North Sea).

The newspaper account ended with the following:

"We are sorry to add that the meeting was slightly interrupted towards the close by the entrance of two brewers' draymen, who were evidently in a state of fermentation."

The Threat of Invasion

Throughout its history, Britain has been protected on many occasions from the threat of invasion by its island status. The threat has always been there, however, and steps have always been taken to try and counter it. The Romans were probably the first to take serious steps to protect these shores – not surprisingly perhaps, since they themselves had invaded and eventually taken control of England in AD43. (This was the second Roman invasion; the first, under Julius Caesar in 55BC, was not followed up.)

By the end of the third century, Saxon raiders were reaching the east coast in ever greater numbers, and so a system of forts was built as a kind of early warning system – a sort of early Fylingdales.

These forts stretched from Huntcliff, near Saltburn, to Filey, with others in between at Scarborough, Ravenscar and Goldsborough (over-looking Runswick Bay). It is thought likely that there were others further south, but coastal erosion has removed any trace of these. The signal stations were linked by road with York, where soldiers were ready to meet any invasion that should come. There was also a Roman fleet of ships, part of which was based on the Humber, and it is thought that there was another Roman harbour, known as *Portus Felix*, somewhere on the Yorkshire coast. Some authorities believe this to have been at Filey (Felix – Filey?), but to date, no firm evidence has been found to back this up. There is a reef of rocks, known as the Spittals, on the south side of, and at right angles to, Filey Brigg, and it is tempting to think that this could have formed a Roman pier. It can be clearly seen at low tide.

Whatever the truth of all this, the Romans left our shores in about AD410, leaving the country open to invaders from Scandinavia (the Norsemen) and Germany, Denmark and Holland (the Danes, Saxons, Angles and Jutes) To begin with, their raids were merely piratical, but increasingly they settled here, making it an invasion by stealth. Almost all the names of our Yorkshire coast towns can be traced back to this period: Ravenscar and Ravenser Spurn (now Spurn Point) are two obvious examples, and it is well known that Scarborough was named after the Viking Skarthi, who took the town in the year AD966, calling it Skarthiburgh.

All of these events culminated in the crisis of 1066, when first Harald Hardrada of Norway, and then William the Conquerer of Normandy invaded Britain; the first was repulsed, the second prevailed, and this was to be the last successful invasion of our shores.

Memories are long, however, and when the American fleet commanded by the Scottish-born John Paul Jones appeared off the Yorkshire coast in the year 1779, there was great alarm throughout Yorkshire, and a real fear that this was to be an invasion. Jones encouraged this belief by firing a shot at Rolston Hall, Mappleton, each time he passed it. The Hall, which is just south of Hornsea, was at that time the home of William Brough, Marshall of the High Court of the Admiralty, and had windows which faced seawards. The shots were no more than a gesture of defiance, but, when Jones appeared off Flamborough with his small fleet, the residents of Sewerby Hall, near Bridlington, fled inland – just in case! Jones fought a historic battle off Flamborough Head (see *Shipwrecks of the Yorkshire Coast, Dalesman Publications, 1974*) but having won the battle, he sailed away from the Yorkshire coast.

In September 1886, Lord Charles Beresford pointed out that France had 200,000 men in her naval reserve, whilst we " … live in a fool's paradise, having only 18,000 – and we take less care of the poor fishermen and sailors on our coasts than we do of domestic anmals … "

It was not humanitarian reasons that made him say this, so much as a fear that we would not have enough fighting men to stave off possible invasion. Some years later, Beresford also pointed out that we ought to use our fishing trawlers and our fishermen as minesweepers in the event of war, because of their skills in handling warps and trawling gear – and this did indeed happen.

The question of Britain's defences was again raised in January 1896, when the *Scarborough Gazette* reported that

" … the whole of the Yorkshire coast is practically undefended … if open towns like Scarborough or Whitby should ever be bombarded, the consequences could hardly fail to be serious … "

We know now, of course, just how prophetic these words were, for on December 16th, 1914, a detachment of German naval vessels appeared off these two towns and carried out just such a bombardment. The battle cruisers *Derfflinger* and *Von der Tann* fired about 500 shells, killing 19 people, wounding many others and damaging many buildings in Scarborough. The shelling of the town lasted for around half an hour, and when the ships moved away, it was to carry out a similar, though less devastating, attack on Whitby. Hartlepool also came under attack by other ships as part of the same raid, and soon afterwards the raiders steamed off, hoping that the British Grand Fleet would be lured into their minefield in the chase that would inevitably follow. Fortunately, this did not happen, though in the ensuing days many ships were to fall victim to the hidden menace of the mines. (See *The Scarborough Minefield.*)

There was to be one more attack on the Yorkshire coast from foreign invaders: at 6.45pm on September 4th, 1917, a German U-boat surfaced in the South Bay at Scarborough and opened fire on the town with her deck gun. She fired thirty rounds, killing three people and wounding five others.

Another U-boat crew actually landed on the Yorkshire coast during this period, but with far less horrifying results: the captain simply wanted to go to the pictures! He was landed on a remote part of the coast from where he walked into the town and watched the film before returning to his vessel – without having attracted the attention of our security forces. After the war, he produced the cinema tickets to prove that he really had done it!

The Unico Disaster

Captain Angelo Dodero was a worried man. He had brought his 364-ton barque *Unico* from Newcastle with the help of Mr Corbett, a north-east coast pilot, who had suggested that Filey Bay would be a safe place to ride out a strong sou'sou'westerly blow. The voyage had really only just begun, for *Unico*'s 600-ton coal cargo was bound for distant Genoa, her home port. People ashore in Filey remarked on the fine appearance of the barque as she swung at her anchor, under Speeton Cliffs.

But now it was all going wrong: the wind had swung round to sou'-sou'east, making Filey Bay a dangerous lee shore. They had to get out of the bay before the wind worsened, and sail was made in the early hours of the morning of January 16th, 1871. The anchor was slipped and they tried desperately to stand out to sea. It was not to be, howev-

er. Dodero's worst fears were realised when the barque was driven by the now hurricane-force wind onto the seaward end of Filey Brigg where the bottom was quickly stove in.

It was every man for himself as some of the crew climbed the foremast to try and escape the horrendous seas, while others launched the three small boats that the barque carried in order to try and save themselves in the pitch darkness. As this was being attempted, a huge sea swept the deck carrying away the boats and the eight men with them. A second sea followed, taking with it the foremast and the six men on it.

Thirteen men died in this dreadful disaster. The bodies of the captain and eight of his crew were recovered and buried in the churchyard of St Oswald's, Filey, where the gravestone can be seen to this day. Four bodies were never found.

Amazingly, perhaps, there was one survivor: a half-dead Italian sailor who found himself thrown ashore on Filey Brigg. As the early dawn light appeared, he found himself looking at the muzzle of an ancient blunderbuss wielded by a Filey fisherman known as Squat Penny who had a penchant for shooting kittiwakes, ducks or whatever other unfortunate creature should come within range! His real name, incidentally, was William Jenkinson and the poor Italian survivor was glad enough to see him once he realised that the blunderbuss was not meant for him!

A rumour circulated locally that the crew of the *Unico* had whiled away the time spent anchored in the bay by over-indulging in alcoholic beverages – so much so that the captain had got roaring drunk, and when disaster seemed imminent had shot the mate dead with a pistol in order to prevent him from spilling the beans at the inevitable inquiry, in the event of their survival. True or not, it made little difference in view of the final outcome.

As a result of this disaster a bell-buoy was put at the end of the Brigg to indicate where the safe water lay; it rings out its sonorous warning to this day.

Wreck of the Sea

Ever since ships appeared on the sea, there have been disputes as to who can claim salvage on anything that is washed ashore as a result of a maritime disaster. The law has long shown an interest in these disputes. A Statute from Edward I states

> " ... where a man, a dog or a cat escape quick [alive] out of a ship, that such ship nor barge, nor anything within them shall be adjudged wreck ... but the goods shall be saved and kept by view of the sheriff ... and delivered into the hands of such as are of the towns where the goods were found, so that if any sue for those goods and after prove that they were his, or perished in his keeping, for a year and a day, they shall be restored to without delay, and if not, shall remain to the king ... "

This statute had the unfortunate implication that it might benefit salvors if they made sure that no man did "escape quick" from any wreck that occurred!

Certainly, shipwrecks were seen as a valuable source of income by people living along the coast. There were even special prayers for mariners that said, in effect, we hope there will be no shipwrecks, but if there are shipwrecks, let them be *here*!

Ever since the Norman Conquest of 1066, the Lord of the Manor at Hunmanby has held rights over wrecks of the sea in the Filey Bay area. But, there have been numerous disputes about this over the years. In 1311, for instance, an inquiry was held to find out what Robert de Lacy, Lord of the Manor at Flamborough, had done with " ... a chest of gold florentines and silver coins to the value of £300, and silver in bar to a great sum, cast ashore at Fyvely, which as wreck of the sea belongs to the king … "

Seven years later, in 1318, a ship was wrecked near Hunmanby Gap and, from it, ropes and spars to the value of forty shillings went to the Lord of the Manor without dispute! More serious was the commission issued in 1348, to enquire into a complaint laid by one Thomas Drypool, a "king's mariner". He reported that his ship, the *La Katherine*, bound for Newcastle, had been driven ashore at Flamborough after being damaged in heavy weather. When the vessel grounded, a number of "evil-doers" boarded the ship and stole 200 florins owned by the king, together with 100 marks of the mariners' money, as well as "... much goods and timber, to the value of £200 … "

Similarly, in 1473, a charge was made against Richard Wellys, master, and Thomas Bent, accomplice, who sailed out from the piers at Flamborough and entered a Scottish ship, *Le Marye,* sailing to England with £200 worth of salmon. What was significant was that the commission in this case called also for the arrest of the owners and victuallers of the raiding vessel, Robert Constable and Thomas Chapman – for Constable was the Lord of the Manor at Flamborough. Clearly he was not above a little piracy when vessels failed to run ashore in bad weather!

Finally, the rights to salvage in Filey Bay were settled in 1864, in favour of the Lord of the Manor at Hunmanby, Admiral Mitford. His rights were defined as

" … the right to fish Filey Bay from low water mark, and as far as a man can ride into the sea and stick in a spear; charge for vessels grounding in the Bay … together with rights of wreck of the sea…"

The Wreck of the Esk

It was a dark and stormy night, September 6th, 1826, when word spread around the town of Redcar that "a great ship was comin' in!"

The 354-ton whaling ship *Esk*, once owned by the famous William Scoresby, was returning to her home port of Whitby with a cargo of whale oil from Greenland, when she was beset by a sudden north-easterly gale of great ferocity. Earlier that day, Captain Dunbar had sailed her into the Tyne to land one member of his crew; as he left the river in a rising wind he was heard to say that he would have her in Hell or Whitby that night!

It was perhaps the worst decision of his life – and certainly his last one.

The *Esk* drove ashore on the beach near Marske, at a place called Reed Howls, at 11 o'clock that night. She rapidly broke her back, and as the two halves drove apart, 24 crew, including the captain, lost their lives. There were just three survivors: Messrs Leach, Boyes and Pearson, one of whom was lame and had to use a crutch, which washed up on the beach close to where he got ashore.

When the *Esk* had been built, at Whitby in 1813, a set of six silver spoons had been put aboard. One of these was lost somewhere on the ship within her first year and, when the vessel sailed on what was to prove her final voyage, the remaining five had been left ashore by the then owner, Thomas Broderick. Some days after the wreck, the missing spoon was found on the beach at Redcar and was returned to the owner.

A Woeful Marine Excursion

Tuesday, August 13th, 1867, was a fine day at Scarborough and amongst the many visitors to be found taking the air were Mr and Mrs Gent and their friend Miss Hurst. As they promenaded along the South Beach, spotting and greeting other gentry of their acquaintance, they noticed a number of fishing cobles pulled up on the beach waiting to take guests for a trip on the briny, in return for a modest pecuniary consideration. It was a warm day, and such a marine excursion seemed irresistible, so they procured the services of one John Dalton, skipper and owner of the smart little coble *Lady Havelock*. Dalton was careful to get his guests aboard without spoiling the Sunday Best in which they were attired, and in no time at all they were scudding merrily out of the bay, a fresh breeze filling the coble's single tan sail.

Not far away, Dalton spotted a large two-masted fishing lugger, sailing a course at right angles to his own, but he felt sure that he could easily cross the bows of the lugger before it reached him. Alas, he had underestimated the speed of the lugger and, as he crossed its path, the larger vessel ripped through the side of the *Lady Havelock*, tipping the hapless vessel over. Quick as a flash, Mr and Mrs Gent, Miss Hurst and John Dalton saved themselves by grabbing hold of chains that formed part of the lugger's bowsprit rigging. Unable to stop, the lugger ploughed on with the survivors clinging on, three parts immersed, and looking singularly undignified! Eventually the lugger was brought to a standstill, but her crew were unable to reach down far enough to aid the unhappy foursome. Nor could they lower a small boat, for their boat had been left ashore, landing fish for the market.

Fortunately, their plight had been observed by others and after dangling for 15 minutes, the four were rescued by the coble *Crown* and returned safely to the beach. Whether Mr Gent got his money back is not known!

The Ship that Sank Herself!

Yorkshire's fishing fleet in the 1870s was largely made up of ketch-rigged sailing smacks, which were inevitably dependent on the wind at a time when many other seafarers were turning increasingly to steam-boats. At North Shields it became the practice for sailing smacks to obtain a tow out to sea by one of the many steam paddle tugs that operated there. Sometimes skippers would shoot their beam trawl net while still under tow, and from there it was but a short step to "cutting out the middleman", and using the steam tug as a trawler. The credit for this is usually given to William Purdy, who used his ancient steam tug *Messenger* as a paddle trawler for the first time in 1877.

Right from the start the venture was a success, and soon other shipowners were buying up paddle tugs and converting them to trawlers, notably at Shields, Sunderland and Scarborough. The first to be owned and based in Scarborough were the *Dandy,* appropriately but coincidentally given the registration number SH 1, and the *Tuskar,* registered as SH 45. Both ships arrived at the port in December 1880 and, within a few days, had been fitted with steam winches and were ready for their new role as fishing trawlers.,

Though the steam trawlers were not in direct competition with the traditional smacks, for they fished in different waters and in different ways, there was, inevitably, conflict between the two. Generally, the smacks sailed far away from their home ports, staying at sea for long periods and icing down the catch. Paddle trawlers, on the other hand, carried no ice, fished inshore and stayed at sea for only a day or two at a time. Nevertheless, when a Royal Commission on trawl fishing was

held at Scarborough in December 1883, traditional smacksmen complained long and loud about the newfangled steam trawlers. George Verrill of Staithes declared that steam trawlers had done more damage to fish stocks in five years than smacks had done in fifteen. Others backed him up, and they tried to have restrictions placed on the paddlers, but to no avail. One impartial observer noted that

> " … Fishermen are subject to two great failings: they are never contented with their own luck, and they are always jealous of the luck of their neighbours … "

The *Tuskar,* however, eventually ran out of luck, for on January 7th, 1895 she virtually sank herself! It was 1.30 in the morning when *Tuskar* tried to haul her nets and found that she had picked up an enormous boulder in them. It was too big to drop through when the cod-end was opened, so they were left with two alternatives: either the boulder had to be landed on the deck, and manhandled clear of the net, or the net had to be cut away from around the rock. Neither of these was an attractive proposition, especially as the ship was rolling badly due to the swell of the sea and the destabilising effect of the boulder. Before a decision could be made, a big swell produced a steeper roll and the rock smashed into the side of the twenty-five year old ship, springing one of her iron plates. *Tuskar* began to take water, and after thirty minutes of pumping it became clear to the seven men aboard that the ship was doomed. They took to their small boat, amid heavy seas, and were picked up by the Grimsby smack *Reliance* which landed them safely at Scarborough that evening. Doubtless the crew of the smack must have felt some small satisfaction in the day's events.